POETICA 19
The Lamentation of the Dead

PETER LEVI

The Lamentation of the Dead

with
The Lament for Arthur O'Leary
by Eileen O'Connell
translated by Eilís Dillon

INAUGURAL LECTURE BY
THE PROFESSOR OF POETRY
IN THE UNIVERSITY OF OXFORD
GIVEN ON 25 OCTOBER 1984

Anvil Press Poetry

Published in 1984 by
ANVIL PRESS POETRY LTD
69 King George Street, London SE10 8PX
ISBN 0 85646 140 7

This book is published with
financial assistance from
The Arts Council of Great Britain

The arms of the University of Oxford
are reproduced on the cover with the
University's permission

Photoset in Joanna by Nene Phototypesetters Ltd

Designed by Christopher Skelton
Printed by Skelton's Press Ltd, Wellingborough, Northants

The Lamentation of the Dead

for
DEIRDRE

TODAY is the feast of Crispinus and Crispianus; it is Agincourt day. When England was still a small, victorious kingdom, at the time when Oxford had recently contributed the word 'quadrangle' to the English language, Shakespeare in his *Henry V* commemorated the dead of Agincourt. The amazing figure of the Chorus in that play, with his inspired voice, and his thrilling rhetoric, has a function unique in Shakespeare's works. He summons up reality, and yet he creates an exalted atmosphere. That was how Shakespeare's audience would like to think of history, and of the heroic dead.

> Can this cockpit hold
> the vasty fields of France? or may we cram
> within this wooden O the very casques
> that did affright the air at Agincourt?
>
> [Prologue, ll. 11–14]

The helmet of Henry V, a battered metal object which Shakespeare tells us the King in modesty refused to have paraded through London, is still displayed above his tomb in Westminster Abbey, and Shakespeare knew it. This play is not so much a lament as a commemoration, a summoning up of the dead. The tiny knot of actors of the Elizabethan stage stand well in their inadequacy for the tiny crowd of the English at Agincourt.

> Then shall our names,
> familiar in his mouth as household words,
> Harry the King, Bedford and Exeter,
> Warwick and Talbot, Salisbury and Gloucester,
> be in their flowing cups freshly remembered.
> This story shall the good man teach his son;
> and Crispin Crispian shall ne'er go by
> from this day to the ending of the world,
> but we in it shall be remembered.
>
> [Act IV , Scene 3, ll. 51–59]

This is the assurance of eternal praise. But the burial, even the lamentation of the dead, is also an important theme that runs through the play from the first act until the chorus of the last.

> I Richard's body have interred new;
> and on it have bestowed more contrite tears
> than from it issued forced drops of blood.
>
> [Act IV, Scene 1, ll. 291–3]

We must think, as so often in Shakespeare, of a ritual that restores the order of nature. The climax of the theme is not only in the magnificent and contrasted lists of the French and English dead: it is also in the renewed fertility of France. In Burgundy's speech in praise of peace in Act V, Scene 2, many threatening and warlike speeches throughout the play are gently transmuted. Of course as a single poem, the play is a lament of a kind for Henry V and his lost victories, though the note of lament is not dominant. The sense of remoteness and loss just touches the very end of the play. It is a praise poem really, as the lamentation of the dead so often is, and it is also the expression of an ideal England.

I felt that I owed these few opening words to this day, and to Shakespeare, the genius of our poetry, and in this part of England the genius of the place. I was pleased and fascinated to discover that this exalted poetry was so conscious of the lamentation of the dead.

The lamentation that I mean belongs in its pure form to simpler and more coherent societies than ours. It is performed, and in an illiterate world it may perish in the performance, though there are fortunate exceptions. We have lost the habit and the tradition, but not the need, I suppose. The dead are lamented nowadays in impure forms. Lorca at the end of *Bodas de Sangre* has a very pure lyrical lament,[1] almost too pure to ring true, yet it does ring true. But Lorca had put down roots into a powerful popular tradition. Éluard, in his poem for Gabriel Péri, a Communist painter shot by the Germans during the war, a poem that I still find almost unbearably moving, could not resist a line or two about hope and the future. No doubt that is forgivable under the Nazi

8

occupation, and I have been carried away, as in the greater case of Shakespeare, by his rhetoric and sentiment: by the truth of his lamentation.

Il y a des mots qui font vivre
et ce sont des mots innocents
le mot chaleur le mot confiance
amour justice et le mot liberté
le mot enfant et le mot gentillesse
et certains noms de fleurs et certains noms de fruits
le mot courage et le mot découvrir
et le mot frère et le mot camarade
et certains noms de pays de villages
et certains noms de femmes et d'amis
ajoutons-y Péri
Péri est mort pour ce qui nous fait vivre . . . [2]

Underneath this modern, metaphysical poem, in which every formality and every idea seems to be an invention of the poet, there does of course lie a traditional theme of lamentation, an identity with nature. 'Péri est mort pour ce qui nous fait vivre.' Odd as it is, one ought to remark that the survival of the natural cycle, the fields and countryside and so on, have often been felt at a popular level to be the deepest purpose of the wars of this afflicted century. 'The shepherd will herd his sheep, the valley will bloom again, and Johnny will go to sleep in his own little bed again. There'll be blue skies over the white cliffs of Dover, tomorrow when the world is free.' No doubt patriotism is extremely local, but a sense of place could scarcely generate or justify a war. 'Il y a des mots innocents.' I am inclined to think that the theme of the reintegration of nature after war may have strayed from the lamentation of the dead.

Elegy is a lament that has strayed from its pure origins. Pastoral elegy, which survived at least to touch the work of Tennyson and of Matthew Arnold, begins with Theokritos, with the death of Daphnis: it is already literary, meant to be read and not to be performed. The ritual of Adonis was an influence, but one would greatly like to know what deeper roots if any the deathbed of Daphnis had in folk poetry. The refrain in the first Idyll of Theokritos at least makes it plain that this is meant to be herdsmen's poetry: but in a highly literary version. Daphnis dies of love, and the song is rather about love than about death. But some themes that do occur in genuine lamentation occur here. He says goodbye to the natural world. He will come no longer to the forest and the wood. He summons Pan to lament him. 'And now let violets grow on brambles and the deer chase the dog, and the order of nature be reversed, and mountain owls contend with nightingales', because Daphnis is dying. Popular, proverbial rhetoric underlies the rhetoric of poetry, and in a dead language they are hard to distinguish. When Moschos adapted this poem as a lament for the poet Bion, the pastoral elegy was well on its way to immortality. One of Bion's characters, taken from two stray mentions in Theokritos, was Lycidas. The fact that genuine and very ancient elements of lamentation of the dead survive in Milton and in Matthew Arnold contributes to the profound force of those poets, I suppose.

In the case of Milton it may be worth noticing that these ancient elements are what lie deepest, certainly what came first, in the composition of his 'Lycidas'. Having written the first version of his opening lines, he went on at once to write down and then to correct the eight lines beginning 'Bring the rathe primrose that forsaken dies';[3] then on the opposite page of his manuscript he began the whole poem again from the beginning. When he came to the place where the lines about flowers now stand, he did not bother to copy them out again, since they were already perfect and legible, but simply noted that they belonged at line 142. This slight laziness has tempted scholars to the view that the flower passage is an afterthought, inserted on a separate sheet. The Trinity manuscript strongly suggests otherwise. Milton ended *Comus* on one side of a page and began 'Lycidas' with its opening lines and the flower passage on the other. The whole of 'Lycidas' then follows in order. This pedantic detail has a certain importance because it shows how Milton conceived his poem, and rules out some interpretations of the whole poem and even some that have been advanced about Milton's prosody. And I dislike the idea that this passage was just an extra flourish, an unnecessary ornament. 'Lycidas' is one of the finest poems in our language, and these emblematic flowers with their freshness and strangeness lie at the heart of it.

Milton strays a long way in the course of 'Lycidas' from lamentation of the dead. To study a genuine lament we should go back to the Bible and the Iliad. There is curiously little ritual lamenting in the Bible, and for an interesting reason. Lamenting the dead has usually, perhaps always, been the role of women.[4] The true lament is women's poetry, and the Bible is mostly men's. Even what pretends to be women's poetry in the Bible often has a mannish quality. Men's lamentation for dead heroes contains boasting and praises and usually some talk of vengeance. Lamenting women are more intimate and more lyrical. Still, some elements are in common.

> And David lamented with this lamentation over Saul, and over Jonathan his son;
> The beauty of Israel is slain upon thy high places; how are the mighty fallen!
> Tell it not in Gath, publish it not in the streets of Ashkelon; lest the daughters of the Philistines rejoice, lest the daughters of the uncircumcised triumph.
> Ye mountains of Gilboa, let there be no dew, neither let there be rain upon you, nor fields of offerings; for there the shield of the mighty is vilely cast away, the shield of Saul, as though he had not been anointed with oil.
> From the blood of the slain, from the fat of the mighty, the bow of Jonathan turned not back, and the sword of Saul returned not empty.
> Saul and Jonathan were lovely and pleasant in their lives, and in their death they were not divided: they were swifter than eagles, they were stronger than lions.
> Ye daughters of Israel, weep over Saul, who clothed you in scarlet, with other delights; who put on ornaments of gold upon your apparel.

How are the mighty fallen in the midst of the battle! O Jonathan, thou wast slain in thine high places.

I am distressed for thee, my brother Jonathan; very pleasant hast thou been unto me: thy love to me was wonderful, passing the love of women.

How are the mighty fallen, and the weapons of war perished![5]

It appears that David may be usurping a woman's role, but this is not the only epic touch in the story of David, and any impurity or intermingling of form may well be due to successive stages of a long transmission. As we now have it at least, this lament is as close to invented poetry as it is to popular ritual. Its heroic quality is common to all the great surviving lamentations of the dead: they are for dead heroes or the dead in battle. They raise the question of an influence of epic poetry, that is heroic narrative poetry, on laments, and of the reverse influence. We have in the *Iliad* a mature heroic narrative that contains lamenting of the dead, as the Second Book of Samuel does, but there also exists on a smaller scale, in Greek and in Irish in the eighteenth century for example, lamentation which includes heroic narrative.

I do not really believe that the poetry of Homer, or Norse epic poetry or prose saga, could in any serious sense arise from laments or praise poetry. Zulu praise poetry, as Maurice Bowra[6] pointed out, is as pure in form as any: it is moving and thrilling, but it never generated an epic. Praise poems are to narrative verse rather as church hymns are to the Christian narratives and the Bible. Epic poetry presupposes a professional tradition. True epic has multiple roots and it transforms everything it touches into itself. The living were praised and the dead lamented in a more formal style, but the lamentation of the dead has a special position in epic poetry as it has in life; lamentation is the closure of the *Iliad*, death ends the first Book of Samuel and lamentation begins the second. The laments in the *Iliad* are heavily influenced by the fluent and flexible style of Homer, and yet their formality is clear.

In the Second Book of Samuel, women seem to be called on only to weep and to wail. In the *Odyssey*, Thetis mother of

Achilles comes ashore with her daughters the Nereids to lament over his dead body. 'They wailed pitifully, and tore their immortal robes. And the nine Muses all replying with beautiful voice lamented him. And all men wept.'[7] The lamentation for Hektor in the last book of the Iliad is fuller, but the form is similar. 'They put him on the carved bed, and stood singers beside him,' [the same word is used for professional poets] 'leaders of laments, who lamented in grievous song, and the women wailed. And white-armed Andromache began their wailing.'[8] Andromache wails in words, briefly, eloquently and personally: Hecuba follows more briefly, then Helen, that is first the widow, then the mother, then the sister-in-law. Hektor's burial follows at once, and the Iliad is over. The lamenting verses are not without formality, particularly Hecuba's, which end with Hector's beauty in death, 'like one that Apollo of the silver bow has killed with gentle weapons.'

But taken together these verses are a deliberate device. They embody and conclude the great themes of the Iliad. Homer has utterly altered the narrative of war to a tragic and compassionate poetry on as vast a moral scale as War and Peace. That alteration is radical, it is intimately interwoven into line after line, and it certainly does not begin with Book XXIV. No serious scholar can ever feel again after reading Colin Macleod's recent commentary[9] that the end of the Iliad is an afterthought. And yet the final, essential moment, and the climax of this vast transformation of values, of the whole Iliad, is the lamentation of the dead Hektor. However Homer may have cooled down the ritual laments of women, which appear in a wilder form a little earlier in the conclusion, it remains true that it was by adapting women's poetry at the climax, and by accepting women's views, that he gave the Iliad its extraordinary power. The lamentation of Hektor is not a stray incident, nor a merely formal closure.[10]

Unfortunately, this is really too civilized to bring us close to genuine ritual. What is the function of Homer's male singers? Did they sing antiphonally? In the end it was women who sang, as the Muses sang and the Nereids wailed for Achilles, but the male singers suggest professional dirges. The closest women of the family then took over, as they might in a village, where I suppose no professional singer might exist. In the Mani,[11] in southern Greece, where the art of lamenting the dead in poetry survived until our own generation, every village or group of villages used to have one or two women who were professional lamenters. Everyone can wail in every family, but not everyone can make and sing the dirge. What Homer records at the end of the Iliad is not quite a dirge, however close; at this point there is something almost novelistic about him. He records inarticulate crying only in the most general terms. One would greatly like to know in what antiphonal songs the Muses lamented Achilles. Aeschylus has some antiphonal lamentation in the Oresteia, but that is little help. Perhaps a dirge was always a passionate conversation of laments with a background of weeping and wailing.

Margaret Alexiou[12] has looked for 'the origin of the lament in the antiphonal singing of two groups of mourners, strangers and kinswomen, each singing a verse in turn and followed by a refrain sung in unison.' One is reluctant to give professional poets so important a role so early in the history of poetry. Poetry is a natural communication, before it becomes a professional activity, and if women could compose laments of great power apparently impromptu in the Mani thirty years ago, and if Homer gives similar powers to his women, we ought to accept that personal and ritual poetry are the common inheritance of traditional societies. That is not to say that every village woman could compose the Iliad: mature epic poetry cannot arise without long time and labour over generations, and it cannot arise without what we call genius. Perhaps Homer's male singers of dirges are a piece of grandeur remembered or imagined from a courtly society, but the laments of village women were all he had ever heard.

Heroic narrative hinges on heroic death, and it is not surprising that the greatest epics are continually haunted by undertones of lamentation. The ironies[13] and dark comments that attend the death of the most minor Homeric heroes constitute such an undertone; they are close to the epigrams carved on gravestones, in some of which the dead speak their own lament and praise, epigrams in many cases inscribed by fathers for their dead sons. These early Greek verse epigrams are heavily overshadowed by the *Iliad*. The father who lives to lament his own son is a fundamental theme of the *Iliad*, and we should think of the *Iliad*'s audience as older than the heroes it commemorates. In Irish folksong the old lament the young, and the conclusion of Atlamál in the Norse poetic *Edda*[14] implies an audience of the old.

> Happy is any man since
> who can beget such offspring,
> so great in deeds.
> Their defiance
> will live after them,
> in every land
> where there are men to hear.

Undertones and fragments of lamentation are to be found in many traditions, probably in all mature epic poetry. In the Balkans, both in Yugoslavia and in Greece, they haunt the ballads and lays (and in Serbo-Croat the epic fragments) of the Turkish period. In 'The Wedding of Milich the Ensign'[15] a young man laments his dead bride.

> Forest of darkness, do not frighten her,
> dark earth, do not lie heavily on her.
> Slim fir, put out your branches further now,
> drop your cold shadows over my bride's head.
> Cuckoo, do not wake up my bride early,
> let her rest peacefully under the earth.

In this tradition, the cuckoo is a bird of ill omen. The young man also dies and his mother laments him.

> She called out like a cuckoo in her grief . . .

In fact she went mad. She watered a vine with her tears and whispered to the vine. She spoke to the setting sun and the rising sun. She was alone.

> Only the mother's grief and her lament,
> calling out like a cuckoo in her grief,
> reeling as the swallow does in mid-air,
> and will cry so until her fated day.

In this poetry the identification with nature is not as simple as it looks.[16] The sun is a death-symbol, the cuckoo and the swallow carry complex traditional meanings, both nature and social ritual are ironically reversed. All these messages are compressed into simple-looking poetry of powerful density. In 'The Mother of the Jugovichi'[17] it has an epic swiftness, and sinuousness, and force. It flickers as Homer does between formality and the most daring originality, with no disruption of its lucid, traditional language. The Jugovichi were killed at the lost battle of Kosovo, which in epic tradition was a symbol like the fall of Troy.

> And in the morning, daybreak of morning,
> two black ravens flying,
> with bloody wings to the shoulder-bone,
> with beaks dripping white foam,
> they are carrying a hero's hand
> with a gold ring on his hand,
> they throw the hand down on his mother's lap.
> The mother of the Jugovichi holds it,
> she turns it around and over,
> she cries out to Damjan's bride:
> 'My daughter, Damjan's bride,
> do you know this hand?'
> Damjan's bride speaks:
> 'Mother, Damjan's mother,
> this is our Damjan's hand.
> I know the ring, mother,
> I brought him the ring at my wedding.'
> The mother takes Damjan's hand,
> she turns it around and over,
> she is whispering to the hand:
> 'My hand, O green apple,
> where did you grow from, where were you torn off?
> You grew in my lap,
> you were torn off on flat Kosovo.'

This terrible poem, with its appalling reversals of nature and of ritual, is surely built on the simple ritual lamentation of two women under normal circumstances, with no Twa Corbies, and no dismembering of the dead. 'The mother takes Damjan's hand,' that is all. The traditional ritual underlies the amazing poem. It was recorded in the nineteenth century from an unknown singer in Croatia; the battle of Kosovo was in the fifteenth.

In Greek of the same period we have the greatest quantity of laments that we have from any language, and the tradition lived long enough to be observed by anthropologists and by travellers. Because this was a living tradition, and perhaps in a few villages it still is, a lot of what survives is simple village poetry. But of course the form as it survived was not untouched by other influences, including narrative poetry, and the liturgical lamentation of the dead Christ. The language is not unpretentious, and some of the laments Passow collected and Teubner published in 1860[18] are impersonal, they are set pieces or special passages that could be reused and adapted on many occasions; that is why they were remembered, to be used in performance. They are in some sense professional. The dramatization is extremely lively and the ironies are dense. Of certain set themes or metaphors, like the 'river of the dead', we have several versions, and here at last we have laments for simple, unrecorded people, sailors and shepherds. Ancient Greek epigrams make it clear enough that the style of country lamentation had always had a simplicity.

I shall arise at break of dawn, the sun two hours unrisen,
I will take water, I will wash, water and I will waken,
and I will take the track, the track, the path so beautiful,
and come upon the rooted rock, and crouch and sit below,
to hear the speaking of the hawk, the stone-hawk's whistling,
to hear the partridge speaking in the voice of nightingale,
where to the eagle she laments and weeps to the stone-hawk:
'My stone-hawk of the stony land, cross-eagle of the field,
you have eaten my true lover and I am left alone.'[19]

Perhaps that is just village music, a faint echo of lament. The true performance of lament was seldom repeated, at least in the Mani. It was considered terribly bad luck to sing the true lamentation of the dead outside its proper occasion. The real thing is passionate and formal. But people were so fond of this poetry and so impressed by it that they did sing imitations and scraps and variations of it. For instance I heard an old woman on a cross-country bus sing a lamentation for the dead Christ that lasted something like an hour. The true style survives best in couplets and short fragments.

> Wake, though you have not had enough of sleep,
> this sleep is heavy, it will bring you harm,
> your youth spoils in your sleep and beauty spoils,
> youth runs to earth and beauty runs to grass.[20]

Gentleness that suddenly turns to harshness has been the essential style of lamentation since the time of the Iliad, and I do not think a fragment like that is the worse for its gentleness. But from what I have said so far, one great example is missing, a heroic lamentation that includes a narrative. It was composed in Irish at the end of the eighteenth century, and recovered in several different versions from illiterate or scarcely literate countrymen and fishermen in the south of Ireland in the 1890s and later. It is called the 'Keen for Art Leary', the 'Lament for Arthur O'Leary'. The chief purpose of this lecture is simply to read you this poem, and to set it in its true context, among the greatest examples that we have of the lamentation of the dead. One cannot comprehend in a single lecture all the branches of this enormous subject, but the 'Lament for Arthur O'Leary' is both a vital piece of evidence, and a very great poem. I think it is the greatest poem written in these islands in the whole eighteenth century. I believe that Goethe, and Thomas Gray, and Wordsworth, and Matthew Arnold, in whose place I am honoured and awed to stand, might all have thought so. Arnold was keen on Celtic poetry, but he failed to discover this, though he travelled where it was known. It is a disgrace to us all that so few of us know Irish.[21] I shall read the English version by Eilís Dillon, which seems to me the best.[22]

The lament was composed by Arthur O'Leary's widow,

Black Eileen or Dark Eileen, but in the course of it his sister and his father also speak. The tradition of lamentation of the dead in Irish is strong, and we have some fine earlier examples. Arthur O'Leary died young on 4 May 1773. His widow was born about 1743, her mother was a poet and her family had been patrons of traditional, wandering Irish poets. Hence the mysterious touches of epic convention and of epic power in this lament. Eileen was an elder kinswoman of Daniel O'Connell, the Liberator; she was married at fifteen to an old man who died at once; she lamented him, and that lament was remembered for many years. It is now lost. In 1767 she fell in love with Arthur O'Leary at Macroom. He was twenty-one years old, and a Captain in the Austrian army. He wore a sword, an illegal act for a Catholic, and when he had won a race against Abraham Morris, High Sheriff of Cork, he refused to sell his horse for five pounds, once again an illegal act. He became effectively an outlaw; he was betrayed by John Cooney at Millstreet. He was shot on the run by a soldier; Abraham Morris was tried for murder and acquitted. Morris then left the area, and died soon afterwards. Arthur O'Leary was buried in unconsecrated ground at Killnamartyr, but later his body was moved to his family's burial place in Kilcrea Abbey. Eileen wrote his epitaph in English:

> Lo! Arthur Leary, generous, handsome, brave,
> Slain in his bloom, lies in this humble grave.

The lament was apparently composed before the second burial, and perhaps for a wake that was held the night before that occasion, which the last stanza foresees. This poem contains many traditional and common elements, and it dramatizes several stages of the story; it is a poem with many elements, not an impromptu lamentation. The true wake would be held in the O'Leary house. So we have lamentation at the death, then the quarrel over the wake, then lamentation before burial, and finally two stanzas for the second burial. I do not believe these were all composed separately; what we have here is a single poem of many elements of lamentation.[23] With this poem a world ended; we had not known that it had lived so long.

The Lament for Arthur O'Leary

From the Irish of Eibhlín Dhubh Ní Chonaill
translated by Eilís Dillon

I

Eileen speaks: My love forever!
The day I first saw you
At the end of the market-house,
My eye observed you,
My heart approved you,
I fled from my father with you,
Far from my home with you.

II

I never repented it:
You whitened a parlour for me,
Painted rooms for me,
Reddened ovens for me,
Baked fine bread for me,
Basted meat for me,
Slaughtered beasts for me;
I slept in ducks' feathers
Till midday milking-time,
Or more if it pleased me.

III

My friend forever!
My mind remembers
That fine spring day
How well your hat suited you,
Bright gold banded,
Sword silver-hilted —
Right hand steady —
Threatening aspect —
Trembling terror
On treacherous enemy —
You poised for a canter

On your slender bay horse.
The Saxons bowed to you,
Down to the ground to you,
Not for love of you
But for deadly fear of you,
Though you lost your life to them,
Oh my soul's darling.

IV

Oh white-handed rider!
How fine your brooch was
Fastened in cambric,
And your hat with laces.
When you crossed the sea to us,
They would clear the street for you,
And not for love of you
But for deadly hatred.

V

My friend you were forever!
When they will come home to me,
Gentle little Conor
And Farr O'Leary, the baby,
They will question me so quickly,
Where did I leave their father.
I'll answer in my anguish
That I left him in Killnamartyr.
They will call out to their father;
And he won't be there to answer.

VI

My friend and my love!
Of the blood of Lord Antrim,
And of Barry of Allchoill,
How well your sword suited you,
Hat gold-banded,

Boots of fine leather,
Coat of broadcloth,
Spun overseas for you.

VII

My friend you were forever!
I knew nothing of your murder
Till your horse came to the stable
With the reins beneath her trailing,
And your heart's blood on her shoulders
Staining the tooled saddle
Where you used to sit and stand.
My first leap reached the threshold,
My second reached the gateway,
My third leap reached the saddle.

VIII

I struck my hands together
And I made the bay horse gallop
As fast as I was able,
Till I found you dead before me
Beside a little furze-bush.
Without Pope or bishop,
Without priest or cleric
To read the death-psalms for you,
But a spent old woman only
Who spread her cloak to shroud you –
Your heart's blood was still flowing;
I did not stay to wipe it
But filled my hands and drank it.

IX

My love you'll be forever!
Rise up from where you're lying
And we'll be going homewards.
We'll have a bullock slaughtered,

We'll call our friends together,
We'll get the music going.
I'll make a fine bed ready
With sheets of snow-white linen,
And fine embroidered covers
That will bring the sweat out through you
Instead of the cold that's on you!

X

Arthur O'Leary's *My friend and my treasure!*
sister speaks: *There's many a handsome woman*
From Cork of the sails
To the bridge of Toames
With a great herd of cattle
And gold for her dowry,
That would not have slept soundly
On the night we were waking you.

XI

Eileen speaks: *My friend and my lamb;*
You must never believe it,
Nor the whisper that reached you,
Nor the venomous stories
That said I was sleeping.
It was not sleep was on me,
But your children were weeping,
And they needed me with them
To bring their sleep to them.

XII

Now judge, my people,
What woman in Ireland
That at every nightfall
Lay down beside him,
That bore his three children,
Would not lose her reason
After Art O'Leary

That's here with me vanquished
Since yesterday morning?

XIII

Arthur O'Leary's Bad luck to you, Morris! —
father speaks: May your heart's blood poison you!
With your squint eyes gaping!
And your knock-knees breaking! —
That murdered my darling,
And no man in Ireland
To fill you with bullets.

XIV

My friend and my heart!
Rise up again now, Art,
Leap up on your horse,
Make straight for Macroom town,
Then to Inchigeela back,
A bottle of wine in your fist,
The same as you drank with your dad.

XV

Eileen speaks: My bitter, long torment
That I was not with you
When the bullet came towards you,
My right side would have taken it
Or a fold of my tunic,
And I would have saved you
Oh smooth-handed rider.

XVI

Arthur O'Leary's My sore sharp sorrow
sister speaks: That I was not behind you
When the gun-powder blazed at you,
My right side would have taken it,
Or a fold of my gown,

And you would have gone free then
Oh grey-eyed rider,
Since you were a match for them.

XVII

Eileen speaks: My friend and my treasure!
It's bad treatment for a hero
To lie hooded in a coffin,
The warm-hearted rider
That fished in bright rivers,
That drank in great houses
With white-breasted women.
My thousand sorrows
That I've lost my companion.

XVIII

Bad luck and misfortune
Come down on you, Morris!
That snatched my protector,
My unborn child's father:
Two of them walking
And the third still within me,
And not likely I'll bear it.

XIX

My friend and my pleasure!
When you went out through the gateway
You turned and came back quickly,
You kissed your two children,
You kissed me on the forehead,
You said: 'Eileen, rise up quickly,
Put your affairs in order
With speed and with decision.
I am leaving home now
And there's no telling if I'll return.'
I mocked this way of talking,
He had said it to me so often.

XX

My friend and my dear!
Oh bright-sworded rider,
Rise up this moment,
Put on your fine suit
Of clean, noble cloth,
Put on your black beaver,
Pull on your gauntlets.
Up with your whip;
Outside your mare is waiting.
Take the narrow road east,
Where the trees thin before you,
Where streams narrow before you,
Where men and women will bow before you,
If they keep their old manners –
But I fear they have lost them.

XXI

My love and my treasure!
Not my dead ancestors,
Nor the deaths of my three children,
Nor Domhnall Mór O'Connell,
Nor Connall that drowned at sea,
Nor the twenty-six years woman
Who went across the water
And held kings in conversation –
It's not on all of them I'm calling
But on Art who was slain last night
At the inch of Carriganima! –
The brown mare's rider
That's here with me only –
With no living soul near him
But the dark little women of the mill,
And my thousand sorrows worsened
That their eyes were dry of tears.

XXII

My friend and my lamb!
Arthur O'Leary,
Of Connor, of Keady,
Of Louis O'Leary,
From west in Geeragh
And from east in Caolchnoc,
Where berries grow freely
And gold nuts on branches
And great floods of apples
All in their seasons.
Would it be a wonder
If Ive Leary were blazing
Besides Ballingeary
And Guagán of the saint
For the firm-handed rider
That hunted the stag down,
All out from Grenagh
When slim hounds fell behind?
And Oh clear-sighted rider,
What happened last night?
For I thought to myself
That nothing could kill you
Though I bought your habit.

XXIII

Arthur O'Leary's
sister speaks:

My friend and my love!
Of the country's best blood,
That kept eighteen wet-nurses at work,
And each received her pay —
A heifer and a mare,
A sow and her litter,
A mill at the ford,
Yellow gold and white silver,
Silks and fine velvets,

A holding of land –
To give her milk freely
To the flower of fair manhood.

XXIV

My love and my treasure
And my love, my white dove!
Though I did not come to you,
Nor bring my troops with me,
That was no shame to me
For they were all enclosed
In shut-up rooms,
In narrow coffins,
In sleep without waking.

XXV

Were it not for the small-pox
And the black death
And the spotted fever,
That powerful army
Would be shaking their harness
And making a clatter
On their way to your funeral,
Oh white-breasted Art.

XXVI

My love you were and my joy!
Of the blood of those rough horsemen
That hunted in the valley,
Till you turned them homewards
And brought them to your hall,
Where knives were being sharpened,
Pork laid out for carving
And countless ribs of mutton,
The red-brown oats were flowing
To make the horses gallop –
Slender, powerful horses

And stable-boys to care them
Who would not think of sleeping
Nor of deserting their horses
If their owners stayed a week,
Oh brother of many friends.

XXVII

My friend and my lamb!
A cloudy vision
Came last night to me
In Cork at midnight
Alone in my bed:
That our white court fell,
That the Geeragh withered,
That your slim hounds were still
And the birds without sweetness
When you were found vanquished
On the side of the mountain,
Without priest or cleric
But an old shrivelled woman
That spread her cloak over you,
Arthur O'Leary,
While your blood flowed freely
On the breast of your shirt.

XXVIII

My love and my treasure!
And well they suited you,
Five-ply stockings,
Boots to your knees,
A three-cornered Caroline,
A lively whip,
On a frisky horse –
Many a modest, mannerly maiden
Would turn to gaze after you.

XXIX

Eileen speaks: My love forever!
And when you went in cities,
Strong and powerful,
The wives of the merchants
All bowed down to you
For they knew in their hearts
What a fine man in bed you were,
And what a fine horseman
And father for children.

XXX

Jesus Christ knows
I'll have no cap on my head,
Nor a shift on my back,
Nor shoes on my feet,
Nor goods in my house,
Nor the brown mare's harness
That I won't spend on lawyers;
That I'll cross the seas
And talk to the king,
And if no one listens
That I'll come back
To the black-blooded clown
That took my treasure from me.

XXXI

My love and my darling!
If my cry were heard westwards
To great Derrynane
And to gold-appled Capling,
Many swift, hearty riders
And white-kerchiefed women
Would be coming here quickly
To weep at your waking,
Beloved Art O'Leary.

XXXII

My heart is warming
To the fine women of the mill
For their goodness in lamenting
The brown mare's rider.

XXXIII

May your black heart fail you,
Oh false John Cooney!
If you wanted a bribe,
You should have asked me.
I'd have given you plenty:
A powerful horse
That would carry you safely
Through the mob
When the hunt is out for you,
Or a fine herd of cattle,
Or ewes to bear lambs for you,
Or the suit of a gentleman
With spurs and top-boots –
Though it's sorry I'd be
To see you done up in them,
For I've always heard
You're a piddling lout.

XXXIV

Oh white-handed rider,
Since you are struck down,
Rise and go after Baldwin,[24]
The ugly wretch
With the spindle shanks,
And take your revenge
For the loss of your mare –
May he never enjoy her.
May his six children wither!
But no bad wish to Máire

Though I have no love for her,
But that my own mother
Gave space in her womb to her
For three long seasons.

XXXV

My love and my dear!
Your stooks are standing,
Your yellow cows milking;
On my heart is such sorrow
That all Munster could not cure it,
Nor the wisdom of the sages.
Till Art O'Leary returns
There will be no end to the grief
That presses down on my heart,
Closed up tight and firm
Like a trunk that is locked
And the key is mislaid.

XXXVI

All you women out there weeping,
Wait a little longer;
We'll drink to Art son of Connor
And the souls of all the dead,
Before he enters the school –
Not learning wisdom or music
But weighed down by earth and stones.

Notes

1   Federico García Lorca, *Obras Completas* (1972), pp. 1171–1272.
2   Paul Éluard, *Oeuvres Complètes*, Pléiade edition (1968), p. 1262. This poem, 'Gabriel Péri', was printed in the collection *Liberté* in 1944.
3   *Lycidas*, lines 142–150.
4   cf. Margaret Alexiou, *The Ritual Lament in Greek Tradition* (1974), p. 212, n. 107.
5   Second Book of Samuel, ch. 1, 17–27.
6   C. M. Bowra, *Heroic Poetry* (1951).
7   *Odyssey* XXIV, 58–62.
8   *Iliad* XXIV, 720f.
9   C. W. MacLeod, *Iliad Book XXIV* (1982).
10 It is interesting that the lamentation of Achilles for Patroklos in Book XVIII echoes the style of women's laments, and women arm him for his vengeance. In the wake for Patroklos in Book XIX, Briseis begins the lamentation. Its resonance overflows into the prophecy of the death of Achilles at the end of the book.
11 cf. Patrick Leigh Fermor, *Mani* (1958), ch. 5, 'Lamentation'.
12 Margaret Alexiou, *The Ritual Lament in Greek Tradition* (1974), p. 13.
13 cf. Jasper Griffin, *Homer on Life and Death* (1980), ch. 4.
14 *The Poetic Edda*, Vol. I, text and translation ed. Ursula Dronke (1969), p. 98.
15 *Marko the Prince*, tr. Anne Pennington and Peter Levi (1984), p. 145.
16 cf. Svetozar Koljević, *The Epic in the Making* (1980), pp. 252–53.
17 *Marko the Prince*, p. 24.
18 Arnold Passow, *Popularia Carmina Graeciae Recentioris* (1860), recently reprinted in Athens.
19 Ibid., p. 288, no. 406.
20 The *Tachydromos* collection, *Ta Demotika Mas Tragoudia* (1966), p. 327, no. 218.
21 Mrs Hall came across traces of the lament during her Irish travels. See *Hall's Ireland* (1842).
22 Eilís Dillon, 'The Lament for Arthur O'Leary', *Irish University Review*, Vol. I, no. 2 (1971), p. 198ff. Thomas Kinsella in *An Duanaire 1600–1900: Poems of the Dispossessed*, Ó Tuama and Kinsella (1981), follows Eilís Dillon rather closely; his albeit extracted version is almost never an improvement. K. H. Jackson in his

Penguin *A Celtic Miscellany* (1971) prints a prose version with useful notes, bibliography and comparative material. John Montague printed a part of the Lament in his *Faber Book of Irish Verse* (1974).

23 There has been some dispute over conflicting versions and the order of stanzas. For example stanza XVIII might fit best after XIII. Eilís Dillon follows Dr Seán Ó Tuama's edition of 1961, but in *An Duanaire* (1981) the father's two stanzas XIII and XIV disappear altogether. This change favours a smoother run, but I think it is for the worse. K. H. Jackson gives these two stanzas to Eileen herself, which must be wrong. The *An Duanaire* text also leaves out stanzas XXXI to XXXIV inclusive: in them XXV is answered, the women are thanked (although in stanza VIII as in stanza XXVII it was only one old woman, stanza XXI has more than one), and John Cooney and Eileen's brother-in-law Mr Baldwin are cursed. I do not think these stanzas are false or intrusive, since the poem is intended to be dramatic and various, not a pure, performed lament. Stanza XXXII is a matter of taste. It seems to me a turning point of the poem.

24 Eileen's twin sister Máire was married to Baldwin, and Eileen first saw Arthur O'Leary from the window of their house in Macroom. Baldwin handed over the disputed horse to Morris.

POETICA

A SERIES OF TEXTS, TRANSLATIONS AND MISCELLANEOUS
WORKS RELATING TO POETRY